Sex

Books by J. G. Bennett

The Way To Be Free
Gurdjieff, A Very Great Enigma
The Dramatic Universe (4 Vols.)
Journeys in Islamic Countries (2 Vols.)
Energies—Material, Vital, Cosmic
Hazard
Existence
Creation
Gurdjieff Today
Talks on Beelzebub's Tales
Needs of a New Age Community
Transformation
The Sevenfold Work
Witness—an Autobiography
Long Pilgrimage
Gurdjieff—Making a New World
The Masters of Wisdom
Deeper Man
Intimations

Sex

The Relationship
Between Sex and
Spiritual Development

J. G. BENNETT

SAMUEL WEISER, INC.

York Beach, Maine

First published in 1981 by
Samuel Weiser, Inc.
Box 612
York Beach, Maine 03910

Reprinted, 1991

ISBN 0-87728-533-0
CCP

Typeset in 10 pt. Schoolbook
Printed in the United States of America

Contents

Preface

Sex is a powerful force in our lives. It is little understood in a human sense. We know a great deal of the chemistry and physiology but we have little to go on regarding the impact of sex on our being. If we are seeking for a transformation in our nature, or at least a way out of the prison of our artificial personalities, we know little of the role that sex can play. The rejection of 'old fashioned' morality has left a serious vacuum. Bereft of rules and inhibitions, men and women pursue an ever elusive satisfaction in their sexual activity. The result is contempt of the sexual act or meaningless indulgence.

Our sexual lives can be improved, but only if we have established in us the aim to go deeper into ourselves and cultivate the more profound aspects of our being. This movement into our own being is the true *work on ourselves* that Gurdjieff taught and it is the touchstone of J.G. Bennett's explanation of the significance of sex. For sleeping man, man who does not work on himself, the sexual act is the natural way in which he excretes the results of sex energy in himself. It amounts to nothing. For a man who does work on himself, the action of sex in himself is of great importance, and sex can help or hinder his progress.

J.G. Bennett, at the very end of his life, set up the International Academy for Continuous Education to introduce seekers to practical methods of self transformation. Every year, he took on about a hundred mostly young men and women. The talks on sex which were made into this book were his response to the evident confusion and needless suffering evident in his students. The book is written in such a way that anyone with any regard for the value of his own being can obtain benefit. The subject is such that general rules of conduct are inappropriate. What is of practical value are not rules but insights into the nature of sexuality itself.

In this lucid exposition, Bennett deals with the critical questions that are being asked by men and women all over the world, who realize that there is something to be discovered that neither religion nor science, as we know them, can provide.

- What effects do men and women have on each other through sex?
- Is there any connection between sex and spirituality?
- Are there essential differences between men and women, not just bodily ones?
- What can a man and woman do for each other?
- What is sex for?
- On what basis can sexual activity be regulated?

There are indeed questions that individuals would want to ask beyond these, but such questions would involve the individuality of the man or woman in their unique circumstances. The sexual drive arises from a very deep place where all our inherent problems are located. It is our spiritual hope that in the end these problems will be resolved, but their resolution resides in our absolute nature and its action beyond the boundaries of anything we know.

Bennett eases our bewilderment before the spontaneity of sex and enables us to see a way of understanding and living better. His guidance can enable men and women to appreciate each other more wisely and, through understanding the role each has to play, to grow in mutual compassion.

A.G.E. Blake   Daglingworth 1980

Introduction

*I*n this book I will be talking about the action of sex in us with little reference to the power of love. We shall have to spend some time in looking at how the sexual energy affects the workings of our bodily and physical apparatus, and the role that it plays in the transformation of the energies which constitute our being. We shall see how the conditioned and egoistic part of our mind distorts and interferes with the normal action of sex in us and we shall also look at this normal action. In animals the action of sex is regulated by and flows into the reproductive cycle common to all forms of life originating from the fusion of two cells: attraction, courtship, copulation, fertilization, gestation and birth are all manifestations of the sexual energy. Man shares this with the animals, but in man sex has an important part to play in the realm of what we call his mind, or psyche. Here we will speak of the transformation and regulation of psychic energies.

We will also speak of sex and the will. Without giving any explanation at this stage, I will simply say that the spiritual nature of man, that is his will, is always expressed in a three fold way. For there to be a complete act of any kind, three different roles must be fulfilled and united: these are the affirmative, receptive and reconciling roles. The affirmative and receptive are prefigured in the two human sexes. It is because there can be union of the man and the woman that is a truly independent reconciliation that human immortality is possible.

To understand something, we must try and see it as a whole in all its diversity. Sex in human life is all or any one of the following: a disease and a source of illusion; a means of reproduction and the perpetuation of the species; a regulator of our psychic energies, or a way towards union of will. All of these must be taken into account if we wish to understand the operation of sex in our lives and what is possible in our human communities. The final chapter is an attempt to sketch the requirements for right sexual life in the truly progressive society.

Sex and Man

The first appearance of life on this planet was not sexual. A thousand million years or so ago there came into being a kind of existence that was self renewing. The mechanism of renewal was *mitosis,* in which the primitive cell divided itself into two identical results. The cells involved were hardly more than elementary pieces of protoplasm which had inside them the chloroplasts capable of running the work of photosynthesis and renewal. They were almost formless.

In this world, there was no birth and death as we know it, for there were no individual cells. All were alike, having come from a common origin by a common path of growth—division—growth.

Such a satisfactory arrangement could have continued until now; but something more was required of life on the earth than self renewal. What was needed was to bring into existence independent centers of initiative—that is, creative beings—who would be able to counteract the effects of time from within existence itself. The disorganizing or entropic nature of time leads to the narrowing down of possibilities and the gradual elimination of freedom in the world. There must be beings capable of creative action and, more, of *self-creation.*

The need for such independent individuals includes the requirement that they should operate within the existing world. In other words, they must be in their very nature committed to action by their dependence on the environment.

These three-fold requirements of independence, involvement and self creation were foreshadowed in the first cells capable of sexual reproduction. It was then that the fusion of two distinct contributions was needed to create a whole. Life— though not all that was living—divided in itself and a new force entered the earth.

The division of the whole into two produced two natures such that reproduction required their union. Cells of this kind were independent, but mortal; they would die. In the union of the two parts of different natures, there was a momentary wholeness only; the new result was subject to death for it had also to be less than whole. This mode of reproduction introduced into the world a restlessness and hazard that was the foundation of the nature of man. In my book, *The Dramatic Universe,* I have called this quality of existence "germinal"* in reference to the germ cell that enters into all sexual reproduction whether in plants or in animals.

The division into two natures that occurred perhaps one thousand million years ago is brought to completion in the internal division of man's nature. This internal division can be called the division between his spiritual and material halves and it leads to the discontent and search which makes his transformation possible. Each requires the other, but something different from either needs to enter in order for the two to be united. This is the energy of love and is as far beyond the range of the creative action of sex as that action is beyond the workings of the energies involved in self renewal.

Between the arising of sex and the emergence of true man, there came about all the evolutionary developments to do with the organization of the energies of perception, movement and feeling that we recognize in the animals.

First there was evolution at the level of the *automatic* energy by which patterns of behavior are built up: this was to do with the development of the nervous system of the vertebrates and the emergence of the instinctive and moving brains essential for the arising of independent locomotion. With the organization of the automatic energy, there could be beings capable of going in search of food and of mates.

---

*C.f. *The Dramatic Universe*, Claymont Communications, 1985, *Vol. II*, by J.G. Bennett, pp. 304-6 and *Vol. IV*, pp. 145-6

A second energy involved was that of the *sensitivity*. When this became organized, there came the possibility of highly refined sensory perceptions and the experience of feeling that we recognize in all animals including man. The organization of this sensitive energy made it possible for there to be 'subjective experience'. It is this energy which renders us vulnerable to our own states, and in man it can be called the 'screen of the mind' in which all his ordinary experience is played out. It is the highest of what can be called the energies of life. On the one hand, it can be drawn into the activities of the automatism, that is into habits and patterns of behavior. On the other, it can be open to influences from beyond life.

Such influences first arose when man became *conscious:* and consciousness is the first of the cosmic energies, that is, of the energies beyond life. When man gained the conscious energy, he gained a mind. This conscious energy enables us to see beyond the confines of the present moment; we can have perceptions which are not bound up with the present content of the sensitive energy. This energy enables us to be free from our subjective states and reactions.

It seems to me almost certain that the energy of *creativity,* which is higher than that of consciousness and operates beyond our awareness, was made part of man by a sexual process.* It is certainly true that it is by the sexual power that man has his most easy access to the creative energy, which is the true heart of his nature. It is the creative energy which enables man to exercise his will, that is, to 'do' in Gurdjieff's sense of the word.

The action of sexual energy depends upon a separation of the sexes for its working. It is like magnetism, which can only be present when the two poles of the magnet are separated. The closer they are to one another, the stronger the force of their attraction; but when they touch, the force goes.

It is totally otherwise with the energy of love. The force of love increases with union, and it is in and through union that there can be love. We should clearly remember this since there is a great confusion in our minds between the force of attraction due to sex, and the force of *love.* In the entry of creativity into

*C.f. *The Dramatic Universe Vol IV*, p. 242.

life, first of all in the arising of sex on the earth and then within the nature of man himself, there was no doubt a great action that came from the creative action of the sun itself; in the coming of love there was an action extending beyond the confines of the solar system altogether.

The Sexual Act

*I*t is commonly supposed that sex in man, as in the animals, has the primary function of continuing the species by reproduction, and that all other uses of sex are in some way illegitimate or merely seeking pleasure. This view is in no way justified. Man has an access to creative energy that is denied the animals and it is primarily through sex that the working of this energy is regulated in him. The normal sexual act between a man and a woman, and no other sexual activity with or without orgasm, produces the regulative effect.

We all know the powerful action that men and women have on each other, but we usually fail to acknowledge that the workings of sex are literally 'beyond the mind' though capable of completely dominating mind and body. In the psyche, sexual urges can overcome all resistance and remove all other objects of attention, and in the blood our chemistry is effectively subordinated to the sexual hormones.

General instructions and explanations about sex serve for very little and any attempt to regulate our sexual activities according to some external code of behavior is misguided. The energy behind sexual activity is the creative energy. This is beyond life and even beyond consciousness. It is in the nature of the creative energy, and therefore of sex, to be spontaneous and unpredictable.

It is relatively easy to see that sex is able to bring about important changes in the functioning of mind and body, but it is not so easy to see how it is possible to control consciously the workings of sex in us. A lower energy cannot direct the workings of a higher energy.

However, it is through the consciousness in us that we can do something about the conditions or in which the creative energy will act. In thinking, for example, it is very important to practice both 'stilling the mind' and maintaining a vigilance in which we are able to recognize the emergence of what is really significant and new.* This conscious work is not creative but it has a profound influence on how creativity works in us. It is through this that we can have the experience, so often remarked upon, of seeing the creative act both originate from us and yet also be something given to us. It is not our 'doing' that is creative but our 'not doing' that opens the door to the creative action.

In man, the sexual energy has a very important natural function, that is to say, a function to do with his existing self. It is able to bring about a harmonization between the different elements of the mind and the elimination of tainted energies, energies that have degraded and become 'poisons' in his psyche. Sex is the established and normal way for this harmonization and elimination to take place.

Gurdjieff says in one of his lectures that the sex center is the reconciling force in the "lower storey" of man's psyche, between the instinctive and moving centers. Sex also provides a general regulating and purifying effect; but on the one condition that it is allowed to function naturally and normally.

Although Mr. Gurdjieff's language was not always the most polite, I give here an extract from a meeting in Paris on 8th April, 1943, dealing with this subject. It came in answer to the question, "Why does the greater part of the associations which interfere with my work come from sexual associations?" His answer was, roughly translated, as follows: "This question is subjective, it is not the same for everyone. It is an abnormality which is the result of childish masturbation. Every man has in him three shits which are produced and which must be eliminated. The first is the result of ordinary food and eliminates itself naturally. This has to be done daily otherwise all sorts of illnesses can occur. In the same way that

*C.F. *Creative Thinking* by J.G. Bennett, Coombe Springs Press, 1975, p. 54.

you go to the water closet to eliminate food, you also need to go
to the water closet for the second, which is rejected in you by the
sexual function. It is necessary for health and for the
equilibrium of the body. For some people it is necessary every
day, with others every week, still others every month or every
six months. This is subjective. For this you have to choose a
good clean water closet; good for you. A third shit is produced in
the head. It is the rejection of the third food: impressions. These
rejected things collect in the cerebellum. This is connected with
piandjoëhary. Medicine does not know of this, just as
medicine does not know of the important role of the appendix in
digestion. The elimination of this is done through right use of
breathing."

The sexual relationship between man and woman produces a cleansing, normalizing effect, provided it does not
introduce fresh troubles. We have to find means by which we
can liberate ourselves from psychic poisons. We can have
states of depression, states of anxiety, states of very great
heaviness and states of anger which we do not see the cause of.
These states are associated with the unusable substances
which accumulate and involve, that is, degrade from a higher
to a lower state, in us from our second or psychic food. They
may originally enter us simply from our contact with other
people or by impressions from the spirit world** and then take
hold in us as they do because of our inner tension and
carelessness.

The sexual contact between a man and woman is no trivial
affair; it is a most intimate conjoining. Gurdjieff, as you may
know, distinguished between personality and essence, desig-
nating by the one what is 'grafted' onto a person by the
environment, and by the other what belongs to a person from
the start, what is his own. Our sexual powers and the force of
our sexuality are properly speaking a part of essence,
something we are born with. Our personalities, that is, our
repertoire of thoughts, moods and physical mannerisms, can
never have a dominant role in sex, but must always be

*See page 27 where the term *piandjoëhary* is explained.
**In Sufism, *alam-i arvah, c.f.* J.G. Bennett, *Deeper Man,* Turnstone Books,
London. In Theosophy, the *astral* world. It is also the world of *energies,* beyond
the world of physical bodies.

secondary, otherwise they are entering into a sphere where they do not belong. Any emotional excitement, for example, about the other person—whether painful or pleasant—has an egoistic quality which interferes with the free flow of creativity in the sex act. Such excitement erects an artificial barrier between oneself and the other person which sex itself seeks to dissolve. Similarly, any attempt through thought to analyze or manipulate the sexual encounter, only prevents the sexual energy from flowing freely and diverts it to 'power a lesser light'. Such egoistic demands are a wastage and distortion of sex, such as Gurdjieff referred to with the term 'masturbation'.

Let me make this as clear as I can. The real delight of sex is neither in mental stimulation nor in emotional excitement but in the enhanced clarity, power and strength of experience on all levels. For example, true feelings, such as joy, wonder, hope and love are not disturbing and exciting because they reach deeper than the egoistic self. These true feelings are spontaneous and are gifts that we can receive only when we forget or lose ourselves. We can recognize this in our own experience, that when sex seems especially good, especially enjoyable, there is a peculiar paradox of involvement and detachment; as if it were happening to onself and yet were quite apart from oneself. The paradox, similar to the one we mentioned earlier in relation to creative thought, is genuine in that it is both true that sex is happening *to* us and yet—and in this can be recognized the working of the creative energy—is happening apart *from* us.

In this free blending of the sexual energy—which almost invariably occurs for everyone, even if only at the moment of orgasm—a real essence contact is forged between man and woman. It is this essence contact which prevents sex from ever being a trivial thing. When a man and a woman have slept together, there is an essence relationship even if there is no personality relationship: there is some trace or record left in the essence, due to the moment in the orgasm when there is a touching of essence patterns, which nothing can prevent.

When we talk, our essence has very little part in it. Our personality does the talking. Most of our actions are personality. When we eat, it is the essence that takes in the food and digests it. The personality does not take much part, except that it may have fantasies about food it can and cannot eat. But once the food goes into our mouths it is the essence which carries on. It is the same with sex; once the man and woman come together, essence takes over. Personality may even totally forget that the event ever occured; essence does not forget. The difference between sex and eating a meal is that when eating a meal only one essence is involved; in sex two essences are involved. It will depend on what is going to be made of one's life as to how much it matters whether there are various essence relationships. If one's essence is not to develop in any way, but to remain an immature essence, then multiple relationships do not matter. If one's essence is to evolve, then sooner or later, many sexual relationships will have to be paid for.

Now, because of what I have been saying, it may be thought that one would be helped by abstaining from sexual relations because of the essence contact involved, and that by such abstinence one might gain some sort of 'spiritual' benefit. This is a misguided notion and is a misunderstanding of the idea of the 'transmutation of sex'. Our sexuality is part of our nature; sex between man and woman plays an essential role in transformation.

It is a very important step when we are able to enter into sexual relationships that do not arise according to the law of accident—that is, through impulses entering our personalities—but come about because they are appropriate in essence. These are the truly natural relationships in which sexuality is not harmful. The sexual urges of the man and the woman can be reconciled and harmonized, without artificiality or strain.

What is required of us is that we become sensitive to what is right and learn how to align ourselves with the impulses of essence rather than those of personality. There needs to be developed in us a special kind of taste, similar to that which can arise in aesthetic matters, that is free of conditioning and independent of external pressures.

In the sexual act, we can be truly ourselves and this should make us very careful in matters of sex. There is an essence-pattern of sex for each one of us and we need to be sensitive to when we deviate from that pattern. This does not mean that there is an inherent mode of sexual behavior which is always appropriate. For example, it happens more than once in the course of our development that there is a real need for some change in our sexual activity. This is true for both man and woman, but it is unpredictable: sometimes more is needed, sometimes less.

When imagination or suggestion enter into sex, things go wrong for both the organism and the psyche, and a hindrance is made for the development of our inner potential as well as harm created in our ordinary lives. I am well aware as I look back on my life, that I distorted the essence pattern of sex in myself by all sorts of things that I had learned and heard about in my personality. I know what a business it was to get free from all that.

For all of us there is a pattern of sexual experience which is truly our own, and another, which we may, knowingly or unknowingly, graft onto it, concerned with what we think will make us superior. This is all personality interfering with sex.

There are compatible and incompatible essences.* I think it is fair to say that if we had no interference from our personality, and especially none from imagination, we should find ourselves attracted to compatible essences and not attracted to incompatible ones. It is then that sex begins to have a fully shared character, where the man is helping the woman to be more fully a woman and the woman is helping the man to be more fully a man.

It is then that it is possible to talk about marriage in the true sense of the word. Marriage becomes possible when there is complementarity between the man and the woman. This cannot be through the personality. It is a major step towards release from egoism and has tremendous implications for the human soul.

Questions
Q. Is it somehow wrong to enjoy sex?

J.G.B. The enjoyment of sex is not only natural but has a place in our transformation. When it is right, there is benefit not only for ourselves but also for the whole of nature. The

*This is largely a question of "type." Gurdjieff said that type is a combination of triads in the essence, and certain triads compliment each other while others do not.

harmony of life on the earth requires renewal and the sexual acts of man have an important part to play in this.

Q. Where does love come into this?

J.G.B. We should never confuse sex with love, they are quite different things. This can be approached first of all through the scale of energies. The energy of love, the unitive energy, stands above that of sex, the creative energy. Love is beyond.

Most people confuse certain powerful sentiments and feelings in themselves with the presence of love. This is simply when sex energy enters the feelings and usually has very little to do with the truly unitive power of love. The result is sentimentality or egoistic desire.

It is quite right to speak of the possibility of love between ourselves and plants and animals as well as with other human beings of our own or the other sex; but because of this we must be wary of crediting even the most 'uplifting' emotions with the quality of love. Gurdjieff instructed people not to pretend to love human beings but to begin with plants and then animals. With people, our egoism gets in the way. Even with Nature, our Mother, we will tend to think that love originates in ourselves. Whereas, in reality, it is Nature that loves us, because She is pure.

For there to be an indwelling of love we must be opened and emptied of self. A special action is involved, that is little understood, because it is so far beyond the reach of our ordinary selves. So long as we remain attached to our own worth, love cannot enter.

Negative Sex

*T*he thinking function in man can be the lowest and most useless of his functions. It is nothing but a semi-animated card index, which produces stereotyped reactions to a whole lot of impressions and is unable to produce anything new of its own. Conversely, the intellectual power makes man the being on whom God relies for the fulfillment of the Cosmic Purpose. Between these two extremes, the thinking function of man has many different gradations. It is through the thinking function that the creative, affirming power of man enters into him and expresses itself.

By seeing this in our thinking function we can understand the same structure in our sex function. On the one hand it is a necessary physiological process; on the other hand it is the seat of the creative power in man. Just as the thinking function can be prostituted, so the sex function can be prostituted. The difference is that there is a more intensive energy, an energy of a great vivifyingness associated with ordinary sex, which is unavoidable since it is required for the continuation of the species.

Gurdjieff speaks of the need for man to eliminate three kinds of filth. The third kind of filth is really the associative thinking, those egoistic thoughts which have to be somehow eliminated. In the elimination of the second kind of filth through sex one has to understand that the sexual act in this respect is simply a means by which a man or woman, or both of them, eliminate harmful products. The sexual act then must not be looked upon as something connected with feeling or having any spiritual quality. Gurdjieff quite brutally says you go to the lavatory to eliminate the waste products of your metabolism of your first food, and a man goes to a woman or vice-versa, to eliminate the waste products of the metabolism of the second food. To regard the sexual partner in any other way than this would be like looking upon defecation as somehow a spiritual activity. It is not. The physical act of the sex function betwen man and woman is primarily concerned with elimination. This does not mean that it is not useful and necessary. It is both useful, because we have to maintain the activity of the sex function for other purposes, and necessary because, if we do not use it, the system becomes poisoned through the involution* of the sexual substances. But it really has to be understood that there must not be any feeling or emotion connected with this, nor should such a word as 'love' be connected with it.

We should be able to see for ourselves that any kind of undue interest in sex is harmful. One reason why it is necessary for us to have the sexual act is that it is very difficult for people who do not work on themselves to prevent the sexual energy degenerating into fantasy. To speak about the sacredness and spiritual significance of sex when one is living on this level is just the same as speaking about the attainment of Objective Reason** or the reality of a soul, when one is living in a world of associations and is full of egoistic thoughts and impulses. Just as it is really sacrilege to talk of our minds as if they were the seat of Objective Reason, so it is sacrilege to talk about our sex function as if it were the seat of our creative power. The mind of man should be the function in which he is the instrument of the Creator of the world. That is what man's mind is given to him for. How little sense this makes with the minds we have!

The creative energy cannot be satisfied unless it is free to create. It can be satisfied by procreation and can also fulfill itself in any other kind of creative activity. But all creative activities are open to hazards which arise partly due to the

---

*"Involution" here means a degrading of quality. An energy of a certain quality can involve into energies of lower quality but greater quantity.

**"Objective Reason" is a term used by Gurdjieff. He describes it as "...nothing else but, so to say, the representative-of-the-very-Essence-of-the-Divinity". *All and Everything, Beelzebub's Tales to his Grandson,* Routledge and Kegan Paul, London, 1950, p. 815.

limitations of our personality, and partly from the limitations imposed by the situations we find ourselves in. Distortions caused by personality or due to the inadequacy of our environment can lead to destructive violence, or degeneration, or simply waste. Unless it is faced with a challenge which corresponds to its own force, the creative energy involves uselessly, and we have now to look at the ways in which this can happen.

Gurdjieff used the term 'masturbation' to express all the ways in which we can waste sexual energy. Sexual fantasy is the most obvious example of the waste of sexual energy, but it takes many forms that are not overtly sexual, and we should see that every kind of idle fantasy is masturbation. People also waste their sexual energy in a whole range of unnecessary activities: talkativeness, over-activity and restlessness, inquisitiveness, identification with persons and things, and the disturbance of the instinctive function in the form of greed and addiction to stimulants. For all those who are not committed to working on themselves for their transformation, masturbation acts like a safety valve for the sexual energy and allows it to be wasted without destructive consequences. For the most part, in fact, there is no real harm in these activities even if the person concerned has a true possibility of transformation, at least in the preliminary stages.

A subtler form of masturbation is where the sex energy involves the emotional life. In ordinary people, the feeling center is almost out of action. This is vividly described in the last chapter of *All and Everything* where the feelings are compared to the horses that draw the carriage, which is the body, and it is said that they are misunderstood and mistreated by the coachman, who stands for the mind. Because the feelings are not given a chance to participate in creative activity, they seek unnecessary sorts of stimulation and become involved in fantasy which is very easily associated with sex.

"The horse as a whole, owing to the negligence of those around it during its early years, and to its constant solitude, is as if locked up within itself; that is to say, its so to say, 'inner life' is driven inside, and for external manifestations it has nothing but inertia.

"Never having seen, in any of the manifestations towards it, even the least love or friendliness, the horse is now ready to surrender itself completely to anybody who gives it the slightest caress."*

As I pointed out, the sexual act is a direct operation of the sexual energy which is complete in itself and does not require the stimulation of the feelings: our inability to integrate our feeling function with the rest of our nature not only distorts our emotional life but also interferes with our sexuality.

Degeneration of the sexual energy occurs when it becomes food for the egoism. Here there is a simple illustration in the conflict of the sexes: when either a man or a woman seeks to dominate over the other, they are causing the sexual energy to degenerate; it ceases to be creative in any true sense and only feeds self love. In fact, the ego in man can never become dominant unless it is associated with sexual energy.

The desire to achieve for the sake of one's own pride or vanity is a great driving force with people, and we should set ourselves to learn to discriminate between a genuinely creative urge and the need to be a success. This can be seen most clearly when people set themselves almost impossible tasks, such as climbing Mount Everest or sailing round the world single handed. Those who undertake such things have a great store of sexual energy, and certainly there can be a creative element in these achievements. When the sexual energy goes into external achievements, it can be an inspiration to others and it can give confidence that man can surpass himself. These are positive and creative uses of the energy. Nevertheless, when we look at such things closely, we can see that far too often they make no real contribution to human welfare, and in fact create even in those who are not directly involved a sense of human superiority which can lead to a senseless imitation.

There can be something heroic in the first conquest of Mount Everest, but those who risk their lives and the lives of others for no reason than to be seen to accomplish a hazardous venture, are mis-using the sexual energy.

Sexual energy can be destructive. It is possible to go from the desire to dominate to the urge to destroy. This applies not only as between man and woman, but in our relations with the

*G.I. Gurdjieff, loc. cit. pp. 1192-1201.

world at large: war and sex have a strong affinity. At all times the solidier has been taken as a sex symbol. The reason for this is by no means obvious; we can understand it if we see how sex degenerates into the urge to destroy. In the Hindu mythology, Shiva and Shakti—the male and female creative powers—stand for these two aspects of sex: Shiva is the God of Sex, both the God of Creation and the God of Destruction; while Shakti is both the Great Mother, loving and compassionate to all creatures and also Durga, the vengeful and destroying Goddess. Destructive degeneration of sex is seen also in many pathological conditions and even leads to self-destruction.

The wastage and degeneration of sex is mainly due to the power of imagination in us. The power of imagination is associated with a certain energy that Gurdjieff called 'piandjoëhary' which is the fifth gradation of evolution of the food that enters the mouth.* It arises in us, as do other gradations, as a result of a blending between the energies derived from food and energies already present in us. The first stages of evolution are straightforward in that they are known in terms of the chemistry of digestion, right up to the special concentrations which are realized in the liver from which our blood is renewed. What follows after, in the stages of evolution, depends on the action coming from the assimilation of air, the second being food, and its own evolution. A point is reached where there is produced an energy of associations and emotions, the "tetartoëhary", out of which the piandjoëhary evolves. What blends with the energy of associations is sexual energy.

Piandjöehary enables us to see, in a direct way, without ratiocination. It is the true substance of visualization, that is the creation of mental images which are not merely internal pictures, but forms that can have a real effect on ourselves and on events. In its highest expression, this energy of imagination is the power of vision. It is by this that we can be inspired to work and to serve and to experience a positive and real link with the emerging future. But it is a two-edged sword.

"...these same substances in being...have the free possibility of giving, in the manifestations of the common presences of three-brained beings, results not similar but 'opposite to each other'.

*c.f. G.I. Gurdjieff, loc. cit. pp. 761, 781-91.

"...That is why, in respect of these being-substances, the beings themselves must be very, very much on their guard in order to avoid undesirable consequences for their entire whole."*

Imagination must be used rightly in the purposeful creation of mental images, not in the indulgence of sexual or any other fantasy. If there is fantasy, the energy degrades into emotional excitement, anger and subjective 'inner posturing' and self inflation. The end result can be a senseless violence.

Once a right essence contact has been experienced, it is not so difficult to begin to work at the elimination of egoism and imagination in sex. But it is not simply the avoidance of passion that is needed. All too often, with men especially, there can arise a cold-bloodedness in sex which is when the power of thinking invades the workings of the sex center. This can lead to perversions, serious mis-use of sex and a particularly harmful form of arrogance.

It is a serious business when thought invades the feeling center to produce a condition of coldness and indifference—or when emotions invade the thinking center to render us incapable of reason and objectivity. Similarly, when thought invades the moving center we become inept and when the feelings enter we lose control over our behavior. But these are nothing in comparison to what happens when the sex center is involved. If the sexual energy invades the other centers they become overactive and various forms of 'hallucination' result. We can get into a condition where we believe that we can think our way to God, or we get into a state of hysteria where we are completely subject to the emotion of the moment, or we become hyperactive outwardly and are forced to invent all kinds of ludicrous and pointless activities.

These conditions are quite general and need to be taken seriously by everyone. Now, we have to turn to the special situation of people who, for whatever reason, do not find themselves entering into heterosexual relationships but are attracted to members of their own sex.

As we have said, love can enter into any relationship, even into that between a man and a plant. And it is evidently true that there can be a very pure love between members of the same

*G.I. Gurdjieff, loc. cit. p. 791.

sex. In Plato's *Symposium,* for example, he shows a deep understanding when he distinguishes between the attitudes of Socrates and Alcibiades towards the love of boys: Alcibiades sees love between men culminating in the sexual act and he expects Socrates, who has declared his love for him, to see it in the same way. He is astonished to find that Socrates is totally unresponsive on the physical level, although his love for Alcibiades and the youth of Athens is unbounded.

It is often asked if the homosexual man or woman is able to achieve transformation. To answer this question, we must first make a clear distinction between the different stages of transformation. In the first, or exoteric stage of transformation there is comparatively little difference between 'normal' and homosexual relationships, though there are two obstacles that can arise.

The first is the sense of guilt that homosexuals can develop in a society which condemns the relationships as 'unnatural'. This, as with all guilt concerning sex, is a degeneration of the sexual energy. The attraction between people of the same sex is not unnatural and even the desire to have sexual contact is not unnatural, though they are not of positive value in self perfecting as the relationship between man and woman can be.

There is, however, another obstacle for homosexuals which comes from looking upon themselves as 'special'. They are very often more sensitive and perceptive than other people, whom they are inclined to look upon as coarse and earthy. The sexual energy then degenerates into a particular kind of imagination which is fed by both partners in the relationship, and this can prevent any real progress. Then the homosexual with a real wish for transformation is confronted with the choice between putting his sexual life or the work of transformation first.

In the second, or mesoteric, stage of the work, where it begins to penetrate more deeply than our ordinary selves, the homosexual may even have a certain advantage because he often is able to come to the realization of his own nothingness more completely than 'normal' people. I have myself seen this happen and have therefore no doubt that it is possible. Nevertheless, in the mesoteric stage of the work, the sexual function must be subordinated to the transformation of energies required for the formation of higher bodies, and the homosexual who cannot restrain his sexual impulses and yet seriously wants to work may have to wait until he reaches an age at which the sexual function beings to lose its force, when a wonderful change can come and a remarkable progress occurs. Many homosexuals are indeed exceptionally perceptive and sensitive to other people, including those of the opposite sex, and they can, therefore, do a great deal of good even if their own transformation is delayed.

I must, however, emphasize once again that the homosexual who thinks himself special or superior to others, cannot even enter the mesoteric stage of the work. It is equally necessary here to put aside any sense of guilt or inferiority. I have myself observed the way that Gurdjieff dealt with homosexuals. He was at pains to give them confidence that they could work on themselves and he never allowed them to feel themselves special.

This is perhaps the central consideration and the most practical touchstone for the right workings of sex in all of us: there should never be any feeling that we are special, or that it is by virtue of some power or quality we have that the sexual act comes about or is what it is. Sex is a cosmic act in which we participate. We do not originate it and all we can 'do' in terms of our own powers, is to interfere. Most important of all, the sense of being special or different separates us from the other person and then we cannot get the benefit of the sexual experience; it becomes simply food for the ego, a waste and a disease. That is why many people find that sex does not lead to unity but to greater separation. The miracle is that though most of us do what we can to spoil ourselves through sex, we are somehow protected, and rarely does it happen that people are irretrievably lost through their indulgence.

Questions

Q.   Surely, sexual satisfaction is important to us?

J.G.B.   Many times in *Beelzebub* you have heard it said that sex activity has become the principle vice of man; that man actually goes to sex as a means of having pleasure. Do you take it seriously or not? Gurdjieff talks about mutual masturbation between man and woman. Do you regard the kind of sexual activity in which there is just mutual exciting of one another as masturbation, or do you regard it as the normal thing compatible with work on oneself? It would be totally absurd for me to say "You must stop having associations of a negative kind and criticism of people going on in your mind," because I know the force of the negative pole of man's nature; so in the same way I do not say to you, "You must have purity in your thoughts and feelings about sex". I say to you: "Are you calling sexual purity something which is not pure at all; are you calling the physical union between man and woman a high function connected with love when it is nothing else but mutual masturbation?" You understand that by 'masturbation' I mean everything that is done by people to excite sexual activity in themselves or in others. We are a kind of half-being, incomplete, but this does not mean that because we need one another, that the help that man should give to woman and woman should give to man can be given until they have learned how to prevent their energies cancelling and destroying one another. If there is no third force, then it must go into degeneration. This is observable in the relationships between men and women.

Q. How can a person tell when a relationship between a man and a woman is bad for them?

J.G.B. Generally, if one's interest in the other person is actually beginning to invade one's concern with the work. Ask yourselves, "How free is the interest and attention that is going into my relationship with another person; is the relationship disposable or is it robbing the purpose for which I came here?" You are quite right to put the question, and I am only wanting to draw your attention to something. With some people it is obviously absurd, they are always wanting to touch one another's bodies, even in public. One should notice what is happening to one's energy if one does this. How can one have the energy for work if it is all drawn into this kind of thing?

Q. How do you tell the difference between what you call mutual masturbation and just sex to get rid of filth?

J.G.B. Elimination is instinctive. The sex act for this necessary purpose is governed by the instinctive center and does not need to be stimulated; it is a spontaneous working of the organism. When there is an instinctive need it should be clear to people, more or less naturally, that they need this, and if they do not have the sexual act their energies are turning into fantasies, or something like that. They are not able to manage their attention which is beginning to be drawn involuntarily into sex. In this case it is clear that it is necessary somehow or other to eliminate this. Sex is a very powerful thing: first of all it is a powerful action that it is not easy to know how to control, and secondly, habits have been formed. It is, in fact, easier to control one's sex function than it is to control one's mind becaue in the mind there is this real root of our own evil principle, but even so it is very difficult.

Q. How can one recognize whether the sexual energy is involving?

J.G.B. One can know it is involving by the color of one's experiences. It produces a certain kind of excitement and disturbance of one's emotions and thoughts, not necessarily in the form of erotic fantasies. They may be more subtle than that. States of excitement and irritability in the emotional center are often due to the involution of the sexual energy, showing that it is beginning to be used by the emotional center. Very often, I am afraid, people describe here experiences which they ascribe to the work, or to the exercises, but which are really experiences of the involution of the sex energy—only I am too polite to say so because I do not wish to discourage people. This work is so difficult that one has no right to discourage people.

Procreation and Parenthood

*B*etween man and woman there is force, sometimes of attraction, sometimes of repulsion. By their mere presence together there is a force, which in itself is not a relationship, even though men and women are drawn to each other to find themselves. Something else has to enter; this can be the sexual act though this is real only in the moment.

We can see in this relationship an example of the dynamism present when three elements come together in an action. All real relationships are reducible to the combination of three independent elements standing to one another as affirming, denying or receptive, and reconciling influences. Because a relationship needs these three elements if it is to enter experience, we speak of the action as triadic.

The sexual act, which is a genuine though momentary union when it is right in essence, transmits the third or reconciling force. It is usual to think of the sexual act as reconciling the affirmative force of the man and the receptive force of the woman but this is only a partial view. From an objective perspective, both the man and the woman are receptive and the affirmation comes from the creative force which is seeking to penetrate into Nature.

Men and women are able to play their respective affirmative and receptive roles only when there is a genuine creation between them. The archetypal relation is that of the conception and generation of a child, though the true relationship of men and women is not confined to this. It is the child which is the bearer or transmitter of the third or reconciling force.

The third force in any relationship has the character of being able to unify the disparate natures of affirmation and receptivity. It is not a means of connecting the two. It is that in which they can become blended into a new creation.

Though, it is usual to think of the 'reconciling' as that which comes out of the meeting of the 'active' and the 'passive', it is not so. The third force is independent and free, and on that account it is usually unperceived or unrecognized. When we look at the conception of a child carefully, it should be obvious that the parents do not 'make' the child but, rather, enable the child to enter existence. There is a meeting of the three in one act which is, essentially, timeless.

In the act of conception, the man and the woman become mother and father. They are more than the poles between which there is the force of sex.

The primary manifestation is in the maternal force. The woman, to become a mother, has the power of attraction over the man, and it is this which arouses in him his paternal power. Looked at from this aspect, it is the mother who initiates the act of conception: yet it is not from an affirmation, but from her receptivity drawing the man to her. In the same way, it is from our receptivity that we draw in the creative power needed to transform ourselves and conceive a soul. Thus, first there is the mother, then the man attracted to her and from their union comes a new being into the world. This is an example of a triad of evolution or concentration.* This new being is a new potential. Something new has entered the world with all sorts of possibilities for transformation. This is what the mother sees or feels in looking at the child, wondering what he or she will become. The emergence of a new potential is one of the characteristic manifestations of the third force.

From the point of view of the father, there is a different action. Conception is an act of transmission. It is very important to realize that a man plays the role of a transmitter of the seed and he is not the originator of that. The creative generative power works through him and carries the pattern of the father into the child, especially if it is a son, who then

*See Appendix II—The Six Forms of Threefoldness—for a more technical explanation of the six fundamental triads we will refer to here: evolution, involution, freedom, order, identity and interaction.

becomes the representative of the father carrying on the line or even continuing the calling and completing the work of the father. The father is affirming, and sees the mother, the receptive, as a means of fulfillment and renewal and a way of expanding and opening out to the future. This is a triad of involution or expansion. The child in his turn can become the transmitter of the affirmative force, so that there is a chain of generation. Without the third force of the child the transmission comes to an end and then we speak truly of a sterile marriage.

Above all, there is the reality of conception as an act initiated by the child itself. Ordinarily, we cannot see that the child has been the initiator of its own procreation, because we cannot see beyond the visible events of the conception. But it is the pre-conceived child who awakens in the woman the attractive force of the mother. Robert Louis Stevenson describes this beautifully in his fable *The Poor Thing** where the child to be conceived acts in such a way that the mother is bound to move towards his conception. The same story is told in Plato's *Republic* in his account of Er, the son of Armenius, who died and then came back into the world after seeing how it is that one returns and the moment of choice involved.

The child before it is conceived does not exist. It is not material nor does it belong to the spirit world of energies. It is in the spiritual world,** simply as the will to be. It is the third force, disembodied. There is no way in which this can be seen without the higher centers working in us which are able to perceive outside of space and time. It is in this spiritual condition that we are given our freedom, before we come to exist. In the Moslem tradition it is taught that before we are born we choose this life. This is a mystery that we are not expected to accept blindly. But even its possible truth has profound implications for us. We must try to form some intuition of this state of pure will, without form or limitation, in which a choice to be born is made, from which comes the act to arouse the maternal power and release the generative force of the father. This is an example of a triad of freedom.

*C.f. *Fables*, R.L. Stevenson, Coombe Springs Press, 1975, p. 63.
**The three worlds are: the world of physical bodies; the world of spirits or energies; and the spiritual world or world of will.

But where to be born, with what parents and what heredity, is not freely chosen. A certain limitation has to be accepted to do with the entry into existence through a combination of a man and a woman in particular circumstances. When the father's sperm enters the mother's ovum, the charter of heredity is written which prevails throughout the whole of the child's life. There is also the charter known as fate, or the pattern governing psychic characteristics and relationships which comes about through the planetary influences which are configured at the moment of conception.

Fate is sometimes called the astral heredity because it applies to the psychic or 'being' aspect of the child, such as character and disposition, whereas physical heredity applies to function and bodily characteristics. Fate comes from the spirit world and is almost as unchangeable in life as the physical heredity unless there is some element of conscious work.

These charters are written into the fertilized cell in the mother's womb through the father and govern the development of the foetus as well as the pattern of external events in the life to come. Their entry into the conception is an example of the triad of order, which simply means that the new being cannot enter the world without coming under certain laws, because he must enter through the action of this father upon this mother.

That is not all. There is a law which enters from beyond, from God, the law of destiny. The destiny of a child is unique with him and independent of his parents and belongs to his spiritual nature or will. To enter existence means to become an agent of purpose, which has no meaning in a purely spiritual world. This purpose must be freely acknowledged and obeyed by choice since it originates in the unconditioned world.

Now we must look at what comes about between the mother and the father through the child. The family is a whole, a unit. It is from the woman, the home-maker, that this unity stems, but it is the child that enables it to hold together. Then, the father can be the head of the family. It is a curious thing how it is that the mother initiates the action whereby the father becomes the head of the family and can speak and act in the outside world for all three. The family of three becomes one identity in which the father is vested with authority.

Looked at the other way, when the initiative is with the

father, we see the mother in a submissive role. She has to accept, for the sake of the child, the particular powers and potential that the father is able to bring, otherwise, the family 'does not work'. It is in a real and positive sense only through the child that the mother can come to accept what the father brings, without coming into conflict with him. She has her own powers and potential, but both she and the father cannot be dominant in the relationship. The child here, is truly the reconciling factor.

Birth is precarious, and the new born is dependent upon the environment. There is probably no other form of life where the newborn is so long dependent as the human child, but this very helplessness endows it with a very great power. Because it has needs, it is not merely requesting, but compelling, attention to itself. It cannot be neglected. The baby's potential, with all its attendant possibilities, exercises a strong influence on people. When it is born, it has already influenced the world; and this power of the child to influence the world then lasts a long time, for twenty years, and acts with a strength out of all proportion to the ability of the child to impose itself. Indeed, we can see that the more helpless a child is—for example, as a spastic—the more it draws to itself the love and service of those around it.

We can look again at what motherhood and fatherhood are. We see them here in life on the earth in its innumerable forms, from plants and insects to the vertebrates and man. They are clearly not something which is special to us people, but it is not so easy to see that these three characteristic roles of father, mother and child are not confined to life as we know it. It is possible that these roles, as shared by most of the forms of life on this planet, are only a rather limited manifestation of something which is of greater cosmic singificance, which is connected with the way the law of threefoldness works in the world. In this aspect, the role of the child is clear enough, as the one which appears in the need, which neither father nor mother are able to resist.

The significance of the role of the mother has long been known to be that of the life-giver and sustainer. It is thus literally correct to speak of Mother Earth in the sense that the earth is an embodiment, or manifestation, of the passive, mother principle in the cosmos, for life has been carried and born on earth as a child is carried and born from its mother. I am saying this because we must understand that a mother is not just a particular form of life on this earth, but a manifestation of a cosmic archetype.

In the same way, a father is also the manifestation of a cosmic archetype; but I have always found it diffcult to understand what it means to be a complete man. If we return to look at the earth as it comes into manifestation and becomes the scene of the cosmic process, the sexual roles appear in a more fundamental form, and we can get a vivid picture of the father archetype. This is quite clear in Fechner's notion of the earth. He saw the earth as a living being, and the birth of life emerging from the marriage of the sun and the earth and very probably there is more than just a simile in this. According to one theory, mutations by which a new species arise are due to special radiation, coming from the sun which has sufficient high energy in it to disturb the pattern in the chromosomes, tending to produce non-viable forms, but occasionally viable varieties of genetic pattern appear which breed true and establish themselves to bring a new species into the world. If there is any truth in this, it would be very interesting in that it presents a picture of the sun having an inseminating role to play in relation to life on the earth.

Thus the active principle should be the bearer of the creative power which can find itself within the world; but for a man it seems an almost impossible manifestation. The reason for this is connected with our particular nature as human beings.

In the Maitri Upanishad it is said that a particle of the Great Self resides in us all, and that it is cut off and unaware of its source. Thus we are destined and intended for transformation, and have therefore to be related to something higher than ourselves that has to be 'created in us'. In that cosmic sense, then, no one can ever be the independent, active principle, but has to be the dependent, passive principle irrespective of which sex one may belong to. So we have this peculiar situation: we are bound to be and cannot be otherwise than passive in our relation to the Higher Power, and yet in our state of existence, the man has to carry and manifest the active principle which is not really his own. A man is thus expected to be something that he cannot be, and I think that most men are aware of something strange about their role. However they may hide it from themselves, they are aware that they occupy a false position and appear to be something they cannot be.

This peculiarity of man's nature actually shows itself in practical life. The woman, who carries a passive principle both existentially and essentially her own, takes quite naturally to motherhood and the fulfillment of her cosmic role, but for a man to be a father is somehow or other only partly natural for him and he therefore fulfills his role more awkwardly than a woman does hers. This is because his role is not essentially one of fatherhood, but only existentially so, giving us the commonly recognized situation of a woman fulfilling her role in parenthood more completely than a man does his, and being a better mother than he is able to be a father. Hence, a woman, seen thus, is a natural form of life and a man an unnatural one, which is very hard to understand.

One can say, then, that there is a cosmic significance of sex, that it is a manifestation of the universal law of threefoldness, which is at the bottom of the reason why the forces and energies associated with it are of such a high order and power.

To remember and meditate upon the cosmic character of the family has an influence upon our lives. However difficult it appears, we are able to conform to this higher pattern and play the roles alloted us. To come to the spiritual truth of parenthood is to be set free from many anxieties.

Now we must look at what this pattern of parenthood can mean for the relationships of people in communities. The relation between man and woman becomes a complete whole when there is the reconciling force of the child; then there is that same everchanging pattern. This is why, quite rightly, the family has always been regarded as the atomic human society, which means that it cannot be further subdivided without destroying its character. This is the essence aspect of sex, but there is nothing in this which requires that there should be a particular father and mother and a single child. There can be fathers, mothers, children, any kind of combination without destroying the basic relationship of parenthood, but parenthood is always, whatever other situations may arise, a unique undissolvable relationship. Father, mother and the child cannot be replaced by anyone else without the whole thing being destroyed and becoming something quite different. There is hardly any other human relationship that has that peculiar quality that it is what it is and nobody and nothing can change it. It does not matter how many husbands a woman may have, how many wives a man may have, or how many children they may have, always there is in parenthood the same unique relationship. This is essence.

It is through this unique relationship of parenthood that the pattern of the human race keeps its vitality; its capacity for variation and progress. But although the relationship is unique, it has the character of the triad. Any element in one triad can be an element in another triad. There is nothing in this which prevents a woman from having children by more than one father, and father having children by more than one wife, or the relationship dissolving and the parents and the children separating from one another. Nothing, not all this flux of human relationships, touches the essential thing.

At the same time, because of the importance of the genetic pattern, the importance of the potential that is created by the union of the sexes, the setting up of parenthood does require some insight into the way in which the patterns can be related to one another. That is to say that if the best potential is to be maintained and the most evolving society is to be achieved, then there should be mating in accordance with patterns. In past times this was not only understood but it was practiced, and parents were chosen in accordance with the means for recognizing the appropriateness of the pattern of the father and the pattern of the mother for mating. Not only mating in the sense of producing children with a high potential but also for mating with the possibility of a sufficiently stable union to maintain the environment during the period of the dependence of the children. People who used to study and were learned in the means and ways by which this matching was to be achieved were called astrologers.

In many countries this is still believed and it is still practiced. In most Asiatic countries, specially those of East Asia, it is almost an invariable custom to consult an astrologer or somebody who is assumed to be able to recognize whether a proposed marriage has the required essence pattern. For some reason that is not quite easy to understand, this has gradually gone out of human life, particularly in Western countries. It is very obvious that the social custom of turning to a presumed expert to discern the essence pattern which makes a union a fruitful and stable one is open to many abuses; like all possession of specialized knowledge which will influence the lives of people. This is no doubt one reason why people have been cautious about it. But I think it is chiefly owing to the loss of understand of the laws of synchronicity.* There has been a loss of interest in the patterns involved and the way in which patterns can be transmitted and blended. I believe that we are now passing out of the phase where man has been mainly obsessed with causality and what is called the scientific method, which studies the way events proceed in time and more or less disregards the patterns that are working in a non-causal way.

Questions

Q.   What did Gurdjieff say about bearing children?

J.G.B.   After hearing Mr. Gurdjieff's explanation of the role of sex in psychic elimination, somebody asked, "I have reflected upon what you said about sex, but I cannot see the connection with procreation."

Mr. Gurdjieff replied, "I did not say a single word about procreation. The birth of children is a grave sacred matter for which one should prepare oneself very specially. What I have said was simply an indication of a way of looking at sex in so far as it is a function which should be free. I have not spoken about procreation. Man should first of all cease to be the slave of his sex function before thinking of creating consciously."

Q.   If one separates the function of sex as a regulator for the energies from parenthood one has to look for the means to avoid parenthood. Could you speak about that?

J.G.B.   I was speaking about that last night, you remember. I was saying about how one would see this in a society of the new world, the new age. It depends on whether one really accepts

*c.f. *The Dramatic Univers Vol. II,* ch. 26.

and recognizes the rightness of the distinction between the first and second sex function, that is sex function as regulator of energies and sex function for reproduction. And if one would go further to recognize that parenthood is an especially sacred thing in itself and that it is a responsibility towards the human race and that people should be permitted to enter into this relationship only if they are fitted for it, then it also follows that steps should be taken for those who do not belong to this category not to have children. There was a certain knowledge about this in ancient times but it may be that with the changing society that we have now and the new situations, other means that become available will be acceptable. The present means for preventing conceptions are still crude but it is very probable that since we are evolving towards a new kind of society, perhaps these also will evolve, having fewer consequences.

Q.   What about polygamy?

J.G.B.   If there can be acceptance, then there can be a relationship involving more than two people. That is the condition. It requires more not less than monogamy. The rule made by Mohammed specified three conditions of polygamy. First, there must be the means to supply the needs of more than one family. Secondly, there must be sufficient virility to satisfy more than one woman. Thirdly, there must be sufficient inner authority in the man for more than one woman to accept him. These conditions somewhat diminished the incidence of polygamy.

Creativity and Perception

*I*t is primarily his sexual power that draws into man the creative energy. In the selfhood and the functions the creative energy can bring about finer perceptions and the kind of purposeful external activity we correctly label as creative. The opening of finer perceptions in us is of fundamental importance for our transformation, for without them we cannot see what is necessary. There comes a point at which the exercise of practices we have learnt, though beneficial and necessary for our development, is not enough for us to find our way. If it were not for the lowly status which these days is given that name, the word "intelligence" would be appropriate for what is needed. Intelligence, in this sense, means a coalescence of creative and conscious energies* and it is easy to see how intelligence is weakened in us by wrong sexual activity.

The part sex plays in artistic creativity is widely known, though on the surface there seems to be a bewildering variety of attitudes involved; in one it is by abstinence, in another seemingly by indulgence. Certainly, it is in no way true that there is a 'sublimation' of sex energy into creativity. This naïve view supposes that there is a definite quantity of creative energy which can go into one of two channels. The reality is more dynamic.

Certainly it is true that sexual abstinence can lead to mystical experience, that is, awareness of suprasensible

The Dramatic Universe by J.G. Bennett, Vol IV p. 95. This coalesence brings about a fusion between will and objective knowledge.

realities. This applies to any restraint on our appetites and some kind of abstinence or check on natural impulses is involved in any work that aims at awakening finer perceptions in people. What is involved is a concentration of free sensitive energy, which is ordinarily used up and dissipated. Eating, talking and sleeping as well as sex are severely restrained in certain spiritual orders.

But it is equally true that the cultivation of sexual experience can lead to mystical perceptions. If we look at traditional practices it is obvious that both abstinence and cultivation of sex have played important roles in the mystical life. In this light, the approach of Tantric Buddhism and that of ascetic Christianity are but two halves of a single coin and within Christianity itself we can find both approaches.

This ambiguous role of sex arises out of the deconditioning power it has in the mind. The mind is the common presence of the three energies, automatic, sensitive and conscious. The automatic energy is the energy of instinct and behavioral patterns; in other words, it is the stuff of habit. The sensitive energy gives contact with the present moment; it is the very energy of experience of life. These two energies are present in all animal life, including man, but the conscious energy is beyond life. It provides an awareness of wholes that is not possible through the reactive and 'self-centered' experience that comes through the life energies. Such an awareness makes judgement and choice possible and is involved in the powers of reflection, memory and language that are characteristic of mind.

The automatic and conscious energies constitute the lower and upper limits of our awareness. The vital energies involved in our physiological functions are largely subliminal and only externally experienced. The higher cosmic energies of creativity and love are supra-conscious and experienced internally as unpredictability and nothingness of self.*

What must be understood is the extent to which the condition of the sensitive energy in us governs our perceptions. This energy constitutes the 'screen of the mind'. In it appear perceptions of the external and the internal world, including images which arise spontaneously from a source beyond the

*See Appendix 1 — Table of Energies.

mind. In the ordinary state, the sensitivity is conditioned, bound to the patterns of the automatism. It may be very perceptive in a specialized direction, through professional training and practice in a certain field, but this is largely in the realm of response to external events, like being a finely tuned receiver. For the sensitivity to receive impressions that are genuinely new, it needs to be deconditioned.

In this, the sexual act plays an important part. If it is experienced in essence, the sensitivity is set free. If there is not that essence experience, then the benefit is lost in spurious emotionality or arrogance.

The sexual act brings about a powerful interplay beween the creative and automatic energies that can sometimes be directly experienced as a shock in the brain. Such a connection is not restricted to the sexual act, but it is the dominant way it manifests for everyone. The connection changes the relation between the sensitive and conscious energies. At times there is a heightened awareness, at others a special oblivion; it depends on the state of inner organization, or strength of mind.

The sexual power in man is not restricted to the sexual act itself. At all times there is some kind of field of force between men and women and a searching or pulling that is largely responsible for the dynamism of human relationships. The sex center has its own perceptions and the most important of these is in the capacity to know directly the reality of other minds. That is why the sex energy is fundamental in the development of group consciousness, and we can see why remarkable things can happen in gatherings of people united in a sexual atmosphere through powerful musical experiences.

When people become aware of the presence of sexual energy where it is not restricted to subjective experiences of the sexual act itself, they can become more open to the inner world in which people are genuinely in contact with each other and not separate. It is the *natural* counterpart to the *supernatural* "communion of saints".

There is an interplay between the sexual action connecting creativity and automatism and the action of conscious work connecting consciousness and sensitivity. The two actions are independent though they have a powerful influence on each other. It is in this that it is possible to find a meaning for the notion of use of sexual energy, while admitting that the creative source is unpredictable in its manifestations.

The key is in the development of finer perceptions into which the cosmic energies of consciousness and creativity enter. Gurdjieff in his system used to speak of the "higher emotional center" as that which can enable us to truly know ourselves in, so to say, 'one glance'. For this, creative energy must penetrate the mind, for only creative energy is sufficiently 'ahead' of where we are to reveal ourselves to ourselves.

The sex energy is given to us for the transformation of the energies of our foods—ordinary food, air and impressions— enabling them to evolve. It is the sex energy that produces most of the piandjoëhary or energy of imagination in us. The creative energy of sex, blending with the range of automatic and sensitive energies, results in this special energy.* It is the energy used in all creative work. If it is not used as creative imagination, the energy involves, that is, degrades and enters the ordinary centers. Eventually it involves down to the vital level where it produces all kinds of illness and disturbance of life. A normal sexual activity is then needed to counterbalance these effects. So we see that the man who is not creative is locked inside the circle of sex. He can maintain a psychic equilibrium, but what is made possible for him through sex is wasted and allowed to degenerate and disperse.

The sexual energy when it is directed through the piandjoëhary into the ordinary centers gives extraordinary powers. This is what Gurdjieff called the "Great Accumulator" and it can come about accidentally as well as consciously.

The energy of imagination, or piandjoëhary, can enable us to do extraordinary things. It is the key to real decision making. It enables us to visualise what *will* come about. It is the key to 'doing'. For those who do not have established the second or *Kesdian*** body, the control of imagination requires a normal sex life or some kind of inner work that can substitute for one. The majority of people do not have a sufficient urge for self perfection to enable them to practice adequate inner work, and therefore a normal sex life is imperative.

_____
*All and Everything, p. ~~751~~. 761
**The second body is probably an organization of the sensitive energy in a man to the point of independence from the workings of the physical body.

What is needed for the transformation of consciousness in us into creativity is the unitive energy of love. The unitive energy is absolutely everywhere and we have no apparatus for carrying such an energy in ourselves, such as we have for the creative energy in our sexual nature. When it enters us it is truly an act of grace.

Looked at in this way, sex in man is the ground of our transformation that which makes it possible—but it is not the way itself.

The creative energy enters into the sexual natures of man and woman and gives rise to perceptions which are of supreme importance for our life on this earth.

Mankind is just emerging from a prolonged period in which coarser perceptions, those by which facts are known, have sufficed for most of its needs. Now, far too many facts are known: we are surfeited with facts and understand nothing. This is the so-called 'information explosion'. I have many times told you my belief that the world is entering a time of transition in which it is quite likely that new forms of perception, completely unlike those we have been accustomed to use, will be called for. These new forms of perception will be connected with our ability to cooperate with the action of the creative engery.

One aspect of the way the creative energy works in people may already be clear to some of you from what I said about the roles of father and motherhood, and this is that the creative energy does not manifest in the same way through men and women. Both have the flow of creative energy equally, but the channels through which it flows are really different not only physiologically but also psychologically. Owing to customs and habits of thought, men and women looking at a situation may talk about it in the same way, but in reality they perceive it quite differently.

I have repeatedly remarked that we must be very wary of giving the words we use anything more than a provisional, exploratory significance, and this holds true here. Very often it is said that women 'think differently' or are 'more emotional' or 'more intuitive' than men, but it is only rarely that such expressions refer to anything other than differences in personality, which have been determined by the environment. The real difference between the perceptions of men and women is on another level entirely, and one which is not ordinarily accessible to us.

In Buddhism one speaks of the 'stainless eye for the truth' or *Dhamma Chakku,* and the 'heavenly eye' or *Dibha Chakku.* The Dhamma Chakku—that is, seeing how the *dharma** is, or what is right—is more characteristically the woman's form of inner perception, and the 'heavenly eye' more the man's. These two forms of inner perception, both necessary and in some respects complementary, are inherent to people, but it must be clearly understood that they cannot be properly awakened in us without a great deal of what Gurdjieff called 'conscious labors and intentional sufferings'. We must also see how important confidence is for their awakening, both confidence that such perceptions are possible for us, and confidence in the reliablity of such perceptions once they begin to make themselves available to us. Men and women should learn to work together in this.

Women often get a sense for the nature of a situation, but when they try to express it, they find that men habitually interpret what they say in their own terms, and either reject it as nonsense or twist it around. Women eventually get so tired of having what they say twisted or dismissed that they end up by not saying it, and there is the danger that they may lose confidence in the validity of such perceptions. A woman must learn to hold to her convictions when she has percieved something in this way. A good deal of the ability to get through the difficult times that are coming will depend upon the courage of women, and as Gurdjieff hinted, it will be very important for them to develop this form of inner perception so they can perceive when danger is coming and where something can be preserved and cared for both materially and in a deeper sense. If you read Gurdjieff's *All and Everything*** you will notice that the only times that the feminine role is cited it is always connected with these sorts of perceptions. The 'party-python-ess' predicts to the rest of Beelzebub's kin that there is going to be trouble of which the male devils are not aware at all, and says that they must remove themselves to a particular part of

---

*The word "dharma" has a very rich meaning, but we can take it to indicate the "right pattern for a situation" or the "law of God".

**c.f. *All and Everything,* pp. 178, 302 and 518.

the world. Again, when Beelzebub wants to unravel for himself certain things of the past, it is through female perception that he is able to put himself in touch with the true nature of events.

Women should work to develop this inner perception of how things are, and men should learn to listen to them. It must also be understood that when a man's inner perceptions are awakened, this allows him to see things which a woman cannot see. The man's perception takes the form of a certain intellectual grasp that is rarely present in women, but it is not the ordinary intellect that I am referring to.

The way men formulate their perceptions, is, on the whole, more accessible to women and accepted rather more readily by them than men are prepared to accept those of women. But women are very often impatient with the results of these perceptions by men. They find men impractical or even unrealistic because, on the whole, these inner perceptions of men are directed towards the potential of a situation, and even when they are perceiving something which is entirely real, they are missing nevertheless what is actually present. While men can miss what is, women, as their perceptions are of what is substantially present, tend to miss what can be realized in a given situation. This is one reason why both men and women need one another.

There is the risk that men may lose their perceptions in abstractions and become satisfied with words or some kind of artificial representation. Men should seek large vision, and strive to realize the wholeness of things, never allowing themselves to be content with the visible and tangible. But they also have to beware all the time of how they can be caught: on the one hand by losing touch with reality and on the other through their own self-love. With women the problems that can arise are different. On the whole, they either do not trust their own perceptions or else they become hysterical about them; by which I mean that it becomes unbearable for them that men cannot see what they see, and they know that there is no hope of being able to make men see. To keep from misusing her perception, a woman must not allow emotion or anything else to cloud it for her.

In all of what I have said so far, I have stressed the differences between the kinds of inner perception available to men and women, but some remarkable people are able to go beyond the limitations of their sexual role to the perfection of a truly human nature, and their perceptions are then incomprehensible to other people. An example that comes to my mind is Saint Teresa of Avila, the greatest Spanish saint, who, because of her balanced nature and insights, had a way of acting that was bewildering to others; men, for example, encountered in her a woman who was more fully a man than they were, while she was also fully a woman.

Questions

Q. Does being sexually involved with many people get in the way of these perceptions you talk about?

J.G.B. These perceptions cannot develop rightly if the man or woman is promiscuous. The sexual act involves the essence, even if the personality is quite unaware of what is really happening. In the essence contact a part of the essence becomes committed to that particular relationship. When there are many sexual relationships, the essence loses its freedom; promiscuity leads to inner confusion. The opening of the inner eye is made vastly more difficult. For the man it will go very slowly, whereas for the woman it will be unreliable and unsatisfactory. The man becomes more dense and coarse while the woman becomes more open to self deception and fantasy.

Q. Can men and women help each other to develop right perceptions?

J.G.B. Men and women can help each other to understand the reality even if they are not sexually involved. It is very important for men and women to learn how to listen to each other and take what each other says seriously. If we really listen, we can usually tell whether what is said is authentic or mixed up with self-love and vanity. Men and women are different and they ought to be different and it is just this very thing that makes the potential for the human race so great.

In matters of parenthood, it is the woman who can see more clearly. She can tell who is the right father for her children far more reliably than a man can tell who is the right mother for his children.

The woman can also see what is right in questions to do with 'the work', that is, efforts towards self-perfection. This is very obvious in the accounts we have of the life of Mohammed, the last of the great prophets. It was his wife Hadija who was sure and gave him the confidence to fulfill his mission while he himself was full of doubts and uncertainty. Even after the revelation on Mount Hera, he still doubted himself—which is incidentally, a right thing since he who does not doubt himself can never become anything—so somebody else had to say "Yes, you do have that role to play". At one time, Mohammed even ran away from Mecca and took refuge in Ethiopia, so uncertain was he of his mission. How different it was with Hadija, who never doubted.

This strength of conviction and ability to be unwavering is in the constitution of the woman. I know how much I have been helped by my wife. While I would be full of doubt and hesitation about a line of action, she would never deviate once she had seen that it was right.

Q. You have spoken about the woman's side, what is the contribution of the man?

J.G.B. In the relationship between men and women, it is the man who has the role of seeing the potential. For example, the man must see whether it is right for them both to leave and go to another country.

In addition to the perceptions proper to man and woman there are certain perceptions which are closed to both unless they are united. They can become united only in the finer structures within them that are free from the conditions of the physical organism. The interpenetration of these finer parts creates something able to see the wholeness of the world.

Marriage

When sex came to the earth, its inseparable companion was death. These two mighty twins still rule over us, but only in so far as we are alive. What there is in us which is beyond life has another destiny.

The sexual energy can enable us to change our being. The action in which we 'make ourselves more than what we are' is called "transformation" and sex is necessary in our transformation, even though we may never take part in the sexual act itself. Sex gives us access to creativity as no other thing does and our self creation is above all a creative act. Hence sex is the key to immortality.

Gurdjieff once said, "Happy is he who knows how to use his exioëhary* for the transformation of his being; unfortunate is he who uses it only for one purpose". When people then asked about the prohibition of the sexual act in certain religions, Gurdjieff replied "...originally they knew the use of these substances and this is the reason for the chastity of monks. Now we have forgotten all this knowledge and all that remains are prohibitions which result in monks having all kinds of specific illnesses."

Sex energy plays an important part in producing out of the experiencings, actions and sufferings of our physical existence, a finer or 'spirit' body, free of the constraints of the earthly

---

*"Exioëhary", is the term used by Gurdjieff to designate the sexual energy. It is one gradation higher than the "piandjoëhary". c.f. *All and Everything,* pp. 791 and 806-10.

body. This is immortality within certain limits; but we remain incomplete beings.

Through the sexual relationship, it is possible for there to come about a unification of the man and woman in their finer or inner bodies. When it is said in the Bible, "And they shall become one flesh" it was the flesh of the spirit body that was intended. The word "flesh" is not really misleading in that the inner or spirit body can be said to be, in its image, like the physical body. This is a union of being and makes it possible for the man and woman to understand each other and share in the same perceptions. But the man and woman remain separate spiritually, that is, in their wills, for they make decisions still each in his or her own way. Only when there is a union of will, do the two natures of man and woman become one. There is a fusion in which the distinction remains but is transcended, so that each has the other nature as well as his or her own. The fusion of natures is a new creation. It is the true soul of man through which he can fulfill his destiny and become free of the conditions of perishing in time and space.

It is necessary for very high cosmic purposes that a certain proportion of humanity should acquire souls and become bearers of a higher supernatural pattern which is organizing and formative, and will act both for the maintenance of the evolutionary process in life and then for the return of the human race towards its source.

The immortal soul of man, which Gurdjieff referred to in *All and Everything* as "the higher being body" is not male or female. It is quite different in kind from the sexually divided parts of our nature, and the normal formation of the soul in man is through the union of the sexes. Some great teachers, for example, Muhyiddin Ibn Arabi, say that it is through the union of man and woman that the soul is prepared for universal love, and that the love of God begins with the love of man and woman. But when he speaks thus, he makes it very clear that what he is referring to is a union of wills. This union is the one which is properly called "marriage", and it is a hard but true saying that real marriage is a very, very rare event in human life, which is provided for only in cases where there is a potential for a particular kind of service. It is only when one has entered into this union that the full significance of sex can really be seen and experienced. Then it can be seen as a total thing, which makes one whole, right from the physical, carnal act of the union of the bodies of man and woman through all the different stages. This is the real mystery of sex, that it has an energy which goes beyond nature and which is the means by which man can enter the spiritual world.

Probably the best terminology there is for the transcendental possibilities opened to us by sex is the Sufi one of the "abodes", though we must remember that here, any language has at best an indicative value, for our spiritual nature is inevitably beyond the reach of all of our ordinary faculties. In Sufism, going back particularly to the teachings of the Khwagagan, the Masters of Wisdom, more than to any other branch of Sufism, the degrees of union are thought of as three abodes, *beit,* or dwellings in man. These can be said to be in the heart of man, in the depth of his own feeling nature, which is hidden from the reach of his ordinary emotions. The first abode is called the *Beit-ul-Muharem. Muharem* means private, interior, or hidden, and comes from the same root as *harem,* which is the hidden place in the house where strangers do not enter. As I have said, our nature is incomplete. To become complete we require union with the other sex. The true union, which is more than an event in the physical world—*marriage* in the real sense of the word—is an act of will, a decision which consists in the mutual acceptance by a man and woman of each other. The Beit-ul-Muharem is the place where man and woman come together in this union, which is the true goal of the sexual life.

It is only through the unconditional acceptance of the other that we come to the wholeness that is marriage. When one has any kind of reservation and bargaining, and one says that "I will put myself second in all except in this respect where I am better or I know better", then this acceptance is not possible. Complete acceptance does not mean subordination, nor does it mean blinding oneself to the weaknesses or defects of the other. If one did, it would not be acceptance: we must accept with our eyes open. This acceptance is a real discipline, and like the will of which it is a manifestation, it is only acquired gradually. When people talk to me and ask me about marriage, I simply say that if they wish their marriage to become a spiritual union, they must set themselves always to put the other first and themselves second; unless this is constantly practiced they will not come to the Beit-ul-Muharem.

It is really very extraordinary that in the whole economy of human nature and in the process of human evolution such a spiritual union should be made possible by the same relationship of man and woman that is required for continuation of our race in time, because this spiritual union is quite different from the union of reproduction. It is possible for it to occur without the sexual act at all and though the normal thing is that it does occur though the sexual act, it is not even essential that the partner in this union should be a living being. There is something that is called the mystical union or mystical marriage which has the same effect, though it must be realized that such a mystical union is even rarer than real marriage itself, and that it can take place only in special circumstances and as the result of a particular need.

Despite the difference between the procreative union and the spiritual union, it can arise as a result of the procreative union that one recognizes that the other person is right for this deeper union. It is so arranged that, on the whole, such a recognition comes from the side of the woman rather than the man. There are reasons for this connected with the woman recognizing the appropriateness of the man to be the father of her children. If, however, this recognition is to lead to the deeper form of union, then it must be a reciprocal thing, must become the foundation of a shared undertaking, a joint committment to achieve this mutual acceptance. Then, when every aspect of the relationship, great or small, is approached from the view of what is necessary to help realize this acceptance, there can begin to be realized, to emerge, a single will, despite the differences in the ordinary faculties of thought, feeling and sensation.

For all this to come about, there has to be a subordination of the egoism. To come to the state where there is such acceptance of one another is only possible if there is an appropriate third force present. I have heard this put very well by priests when a couple come to be married: "You come to be married as two, but now you are three because Christ is making the third, and now you are three with Christ, through Christ you can be one." But if we do not like to use this language—because we feel somehow that it has become debased—then, using our language we speak of the third force necessary for this union as 'the Work'.

This is difficult to understand. We can see the visible differences between a couple, the sorts of conflicts that arise in their external relationship. When our work on ourselves gains a certain momentum we may even begin to perceive the sort of psychic differences I spoke about when I discussed the inner perceptions. But more deeply still, and quite beyond anything we ourselves can experience—as we are accustomed to use the word—there are still conflicting forces at work between man and woman, which cannot be reconciled as long as they are not of one will. It is my conviction that it is virtually impossible to have marriage in the true sense without the Work, because only the Work can serve to reconcile these inmost conflicting forces. It is not that these conflicting forces disappear. Instead, they are reconciled in such a way that the three become one, such that the Work is really incarnated in them. When a complete acceptance of one another has been made possible in this way, there comes a certain moment in the evolution of the sexual life when this inner unity of will becomes unmistakable, and it is clear that there is no domination by the one over the other and their decisions are identical. They may become aware, for example, that their thought now is often the same, or that their perceptions have broadened to the point that when they look at something they recognize that they have seen the same thing. Most important, however, is the certainty that they are able, and in fact, do accept the whole of the relationship, and, very simply, each is completely free while at the same time there is a complete union of the two as one. The awareness that there is no demand and no possessiveness and the recognition that there is an identity of will are all indications that the Beit-ul-Muharem has been opened.

A further stage in this inner evolution of the sexual life is reached when the man and woman, having created in themselves the required 'ableness-to-be', go, in a further act of acceptance, from the Beit-ul-Muharem into the *Beit-ul-Muka-des*. In this place, others may enter. It is more than a private dwelling place. The word *Mukades* means sacred and when a man and woman have entered in here they have become altogether different from anyone we can know ordinarily. In Buddhism, for example, one who has entered into this abode is described as the *bodhisattva*.

Having transcended themselves, the man and woman are able to enter into an acceptance of the human race which Gurdjieff described as 'impartial love', in which *all* people are accepted inwardly as they accepted each other in the Beit-ul-Muharem.

In considering the union of men and women there is a single thread throughout. This is acceptance. We should not be timid in front of sex and think that the only reality that means anything is the ultimate union in which the truly sacred aspect of sex is realized. Even without what I call total acceptance, there can be a transient acceptance, a moment in which a man and a woman have no conscious reserve or withholding from one another. If it is only transient, it remains only as a memory; leading people to try to resume it again, which they cannot do, for the creative energy is not at our command.

There can be a very strong attraction between a man and a woman, even love; yet within, in their consciousness, they are aware that there is not a total and unreserved acceptance. Anything less than total acceptance will not realize the extraordinary potential of our human nature. It requires sacrifice, not the superficial sacrifice of one's interests or inclinations, but the sacrifice of oneself and a willingness not to be oneself but to be ourselves.

It is a great tragedy when people who are capable of the act of marriage, miss the opportunity because they do not know what is required, what the secret is. Marriage is a great step in one's transformation, but if a man and woman are able to accept one another totally, they are very close to being able to accept all other people as well. That is why it is said that there cannot be such a thing as partial love: if anyone truly loves, they love everyone, love all. Those who enter into marriage by that act alone do great service for humanity.

The transient acceptance gives us a taste of what is possible. We know how love spills over and we love everything we look at; for a moment, the egoism is suspended. For that to be made permanent, a long and arduous way has to be followed. We must needs be humiliated in ourselves to admit the higher love that makes it possible.

The condition of union is spiritual. To understand this we have to reverse our ordinary view of reality. In the common view, the substantial reality we have is that of our bodies, within which we can come to experience an 'inner world' of energies. Then somehow beyond that, it is believed there lies the spiritual world of will and principles. But the reverse is the case. Our reality is not in having this body, nor even this nature or being, but in that we are incarnations of a principle of the spiritual or third world. This world is the world of the names of God, *esmâ,* as referred to by Ibn Arabi.

Man is made in "the image of God" because spiritual principles are expressed in him. The threefoldness of a complete act of will, or the triad, is reflected in our nature. Man has three primary brains each of which transmits one of the three impulses. In the relationship of husband and wife, the man and woman can realize their affirmative and receptive roles because there can be the Work to reconcile them. The Work here is that action which has been given to man to enable him to co-operate with the higher powers.

The whole cosmos is moving towards unity and integration, from a state of dispersal towards a higher state of organization whereby a new creation is set free. This is the spiritualization of matter and the realization of the spirit.

Man is an evolving species. It is not in his nature to stand still. As an individual he can enter the stream of spiritualization and realization and be transformed. Unless he is transformed, he is no more than an animal and like an animal, will one day cease to exist.

The transformation of man is not a private affair, nor is the transformation of the species the product of a number of discrete perfected individuals, separate from each other. Man as a whole is moving towards unity. As far as we can say that there is a goal of human evolution, it is that the entire human race should become one organized individual with one total experience. How many millions of years that will take, nobody knows.

Sex and Society

*I*f we take into account all that has been said about the realities of sex, we can easily see that the way in which sex is regulated in contemporary society is quite unrealistic and misguided. There are two main facts we must be clear about. First of all, that the primary normative function of sex for most people is neither procreation nor pleasure, but the regulation of psychic energies. Secondly, that true marriage or union is possible only for the few who are able and willing to make the sacrifice of self involved. These facts are completely ignored in the structures of our society. What I propose to do here is to outline what structures ought to be established to correspond with the facts of human sex.

The primary sexual function is the sexual act between man and woman, which as we have said, regulates of itself the flow of the creative energy through us, as well as allowing the elimination of substances which are formed from all our psychic activities. Those who, during the period of sexual vigor, are not able to have the normal sexual function, suffer a disturbance of all of these energies, and provision would have to be made for sexual acts between men and women solely with these regulative purposes in mind.

There is what can be called a 'transient relationship' between men and women—one can say 'without a before or after'—which is quite normal, simply concerned with the regulation of energy. It seems to me that, at the present time, the tendency towards such 'transient unions' between young men and women is desirable and very much in accordance with the needs of a normal sexuality. In some societies, provision was made for such transient relationships; in our present society they are provided for, as it were, under the counter, but not always so far under. It is very important, however, that we clearly distinguish between 'transient relationships', as I have used that phrase, and promiscuous relationships. Promiscuous relationships are almost entirely for the satisfaction of personality, while the transient union takes into account the blending of essences.

We do not realize the extent to which the present world malaise is due to all the tensions that arise because of ignorance about patterns and the way in which the fates of people can be mutually favorable or destructive. As it seems unlikely that the predictive science of astrology, which at one time was able to tell the compatibility of essences, will develop again, we have to try to see what is a possible transition from our present chaotic state of affairs to one which could better fulfill man's true nature and potential. It is not by any outward signs that we can come to recognize what is required here, for the simple reason, again, that the sex function belongs to essence. There is in all of us the potential of a certain inner perception which can be awakened to provide the direction our sexuality must have if it is to regulate our energies while avoiding destructive essence involvements. We can use Gurdjieff's words 'organic-self-shame' to refer to this perception, which is connected to the action in us of conscience.

We can picture to ourselves a kind of social arrangement in which there is a provisional, almost contractual, relationship of cohabitation, which is understood not to be marriage, and which does not contain the provisions nowadays attached to the 'marriage of permanence': indissolubility and exclusivity. We must realize, however, that such a state of affairs is only feasible given a certain committment to work on oneself, as it is only through such work that the perceptions necessary to rightly guide such relationships, can be formed. Then, out of such transient relationships can arise permanent essence relationships of the kind which are needed to raise families under genuinely favorable conditions, and this leads into the next function of sex.

Procreation is the second sexual function and it must be

understood quite separately as it requires certain special considerations which the first does not. As I said earlier, the parents have a responsibility towards the child which begins before its conception and continues until it reaches the age of independence, and implicit in this responsibility is the necessity of a stable and enduring relationship. Traditionally, this stability was provided by the social structure through all the elaborate customs, laws and rules about mating, but nowadays it is becoming apparent that such externally imposed stability is in many ways unsatisfactory. To see why this should be so, we will have to see what is entailed in this procreative sexual relationship.

Our inability to confront the procreative relationship even on the simplest, most basic levels, is fairly complete, while we remain deeply ignorant of its more essential aspects. Something of the importance of procreation may become apparent if we reflect that the future of the human race is held in the mating of men and women. What this implies is that, because of its importance for the race as a whole, procreation should be carefully regulated. In ancient, traditional communities, procreation was not only regarded as a sacred act, but one that required for its regulation knowledge of a sort not accessible to ordinary people.

The original astrologer-physicians who were really capable of this knowledge, understood the science of service, that is, how to transform the results of one's own suffering into a benefit for others. It was by this that the astrologer was able to perform his work, not simply by the possession of information and skills.

Parenthood is the most obvious example of what Gurdjieff meant by "intentional suffering", that is, undergoing suffering for the benefit of others. Every parent knows how it is that the only way to play that role is not to expect any reward or comfort but simply to do what is right for the child. It is difficult work and suffering comes; but it is a most important kind of work which greatly helps our transformation.

It should be understood that there is an essence union between men and women which is concerned not only with the actualization of the pattern of generation, that is, with the pattern of childbearing, but also with the pattern of human relationship itself and the living of a full productive life between man and woman in which each contributes to the enrichment of the life of the other. The conditions which allow a man and woman to create this sort of union for themselves are the same as are required if they are to be worthy to participate in the procreative process, that is, there must be a genuine committment towards their shared transformation. When people come and talk to me about getting married I do try to make this point clear, because this is a self evident matter for me. In hundreds and thousands of marriages I have seen for myself how seldom it is that a marriage is really stable, not just externally, without this higher aim in which the father and mother share. This sort of union, which is on the essence level, is something very few arrive at, yet it has no pretentions of belonging to the spiritual marriage.

As regards the second sexual function, an indiscriminate mating means the production of an indiscriminate breed. It is a strange thing, which many people have noted, that we modern people breed almost indiscriminately, without reference to genetic considerations. For a hundred years now, we have been in possession of a great deal of knowledge about genetics and the rules for successful breeding which we apply with increasing success to almost every species of plant and animal life with which we have concern, except our own. So we are able to produce greatly improved grains, fruits, flowers and animals of almost any kind that we require; and yet with the human race, on the whole we do the opposite and with the indiscriminate mating of men and women which is customary we encourage the proliferation of the less stable genetic patterns and breed out the ones with higher qualities.

On a deeper level, human beings have shown that they are inherently inwardly unstable and incapable of making any sort of long commitment which is required for the normal procreative union. Worse, they are very often insensitive to what should be the guiding force in such a relationship, which arises and manifests itself through the need of the child; or rather, we can say that they are sensitive in the wrong way, because they do not see what the child objectively needs, but approach him solely from their preconceptions of what he should be like, or what they want him to be like. We can see this very clearly with newborn children, how people construct for them an imagined personality and attach thoughts and desires to their actions when it is likely that no such experience is even possible yet on the child's own part. In a normal society people would not be allowed to enter into this kind of relationship unless they had shown that they were able to make a commitment which includes a certain acceptance of the need to work on themselves in order to achieve the required stability and sensitivity.

Presently, the avoidance of involuntary conception seems to be becoming a possibility without the disturbance of energies. This has not yet been achieved at the moment. The methods that prevent conception have undesirable psychological and physical consequences, but new means may become available.

But there is no sign that people would be prepared to accept the kind of discipline involved in making the stable family relationship something permissible only for people who are prepared to make the commitment and accept the discipline connected with intensive work on oneself. One result of this is that we diminish the chances that children with higher potential will be born. This is a rather serious thing at the present time when children with higher potential need to be born in greater proportion than at other times, because of the crisis through which the world is passing and the extreme need for people with spiritual development. It can even be thought of in the terms used by Dr. Bidder, a professor of biology at Cambridge, in an argument with a number of other zoologists about the decay of the spiritual life in the West. He explained that, very simply, the advocacy of a celibate life for spiritual people means that for 2,000 years we have systematically bred out of our race people with spiritual potential. This does not mean that a child with the potential for a soul with a very high destiny is visibly or invariably born into a propitious situation, but clearly, parents of recognizable spiritual attainments would, at the very least, tend to bear a greater proportion of children with the potential for forming relatively pure souls, with less hereditary taint. Just such an objective was aimed at in ancient times through the services of the astrologers.

As for the third sexual function, we can see that it plays

virtually no part in today's world. We have taken old traditions and have not looked at their relevance for a modern society. Our monogamous system, with one man and one woman permanently mated, very seldom works in practice because we have taken the kernel of truth—that marriage is one of the most sacred things in human life—and misinterpreted it, turned it into something utterly degrading by the imposition on people of a pattern of life where there is no corresponding inner reality. Marriage in the true sense, that is, the indissoluble union between male and female, active and passive principles, represents the very pinnacle of human life, and cannot be demanded of those who are not capable of it. It is not merely wrong, but even impious, to fasten onto people a label which they are not capable of bearing, and the awkwardness of our present social arrangement is that it is based, not only on a misunderstanding of human nature, but also on an even more serious misunderstanding of spiritual reality.

If the regulative and procreative roles of sex could be rightly established, then marriage could be seen for what it truly is. It would be understood by all to be a source of blessing for all mankind. Blessing is an objective action whereby spiritual power reaches into the existing world to renew faith, hope and love. Without this blessing, human life becomes insufferable. The true marriage is the very kernel of human unity and any society that even approximates to the spiritual pattern of humankind, needs some, even if only very few, such unions.

The union of man and woman comes about to fulfill a common destiny. The two are one in the secret place, even though they may be separate in time and space. When this place opens in love towards all, all who are surrendered to love, may enter. It is the communion of saints, an inner society, which brings into the presence of mankind the influence of what, in time, is the far distant future of mankind when all will be in communion.

There is a union even beyond this. In the Sufi terminology we have been using it is called the *Beit-ul-Ma'mour,* or the Abode of the Lord. In this union, God enters the soul. This is the same as saying that the supernatural reality beyond the limits of the Solar System is immediately present in the Sacred

Marriage. Whereas the first abode, the Beit-ul-Muharem, is a union on the level of conscious energy, and the second the Beit-ul-Mukades is a union on the level of the creative energy; the third union is on the level of the energy of love. The supernatural reality of the third cosmic or reconciling force can manifest directly. It makes possible a redemptive action, unconstrained by any limitations of space, time and number. God enters into the marriage as the child and the source of their union. In the Beit-ul-Ma'mour the man and the woman have lost the illusion of their separate existence; they have even lost entirely the illusion of existing at all.

APPENDIX I
*Table of Energies**

Cosmic	TRANSCENDENT	Ultimate energy. Prime mover.
	UNITIVE	Love. Union without distinction.
	CREATIVE	Spontaneity. Medium of the will. Energy of sex. Supra-conscious.
	CONSCIOUS	Direct perception. Power of choice. Whole-awareness.
Vital	SENSITIVE	Screen of the mind. Awareness of parts. Indirect perception.
	AUTOMATIC	Conditioned behaviour. Instinct. Subconscious.
	VITAL	Life force. Energy of physiological regeneration.
	CONSTRUCTIVE	Organisation of elementary systems. Self-renewal.
Material	PLASTIC	Changes of form.
	COHESIVE	Rigidity in solids. Surface tension.
	DIRECTED	Electricity, gravitation, etc.
	DISPERSED	Heat. Random motion.

*For a more detailed explanation, the interested reader should study *Energies, Material, Vital, Cosmic,* by J.G. Bennett, Coombe Springs Press, 1975.

APPENDIX I

Characteristics of energies of particular relevance to the discussion of this book.

	absoluteness	
UNITIVE	*Union*	love
	illumination	
CREATIVE	*Individuality*	sexual energy
	intelligence	
CONSCIOUS	*Understanding*	acceptance, commitment
	mentality	
SENSITIVE	*Essence*	natural pattern of life
	reactions	
AUTOMATIC	*Personality*	conditioning of thought, behaviour and feelings.
	physiology	
VITAL	*Germ cell*	urge to live
	growth	
CONSTRUCTIVE	*Chromosomes*	meiosis
	anatomy	

The Six Forms of Threefoldness

We say that for something to happen there must be:

1. an affirming or 'driving' force
2. an receptive or 'giving-way' force
3. a third or reconciling force which enables the active and passive to enter into a union

We are used to believing that everything works as if it were all started by affirming or driving forces. Yet if we look at a country in which there is a ruler (1) and the ruled (2) we cannot maintain that all change and action is initiated always by the ruler. Actions originate from the populace but they do not lose their passive role. A cry for justice reveals a state of dependency. There are also actions from the intelligentsia and middle leaders (3) who keep the system of government together. They initiate reforms, adjust the balance of power, and introduce new ideas.

Thus, we say that any of the three forces can initiate an action.

Also, the result of an action can be felt or brought about in any of the other two forces. Thus there can be two sorts of action intiated by each of the forces. When we work it out, there are just six possible forms:

$$1 - 2 - 3 \quad 2 - 1 - 3 \quad 3 - 2 - 1$$
$$1 - 3 - 2 \quad 2 - 3 - 1 \quad 3 - 1 - 2$$

where the first number indicates the force which takes the initiative and the last one where the action is manifest.

$1 - 2 - 3$ *Triad of Expansion* (or Involution) (see p. 34). The active force enters into the receptive to produce reconciling results. What happens is a blending in which the active force loses some of its original power while gaining range and expression. The outcome is that the third force transmits the modified character of the active force. Something of the original potential is lost in manifestation.

The child is made in the image of the father but is formed in the mother.

2 — 1 — 3 *Triad of Evolution* (or Concentration) (see p. 34). The receptive force initiates the action by attraction. The result is a new potential. It is the opposite to involution where there is loss of potential. Without evolution everything would run down and disperse.

The future of the race is in the inner wisdom of women. Though they cannot bring about the new conception, they can discern the right father. The power of the receptive force is largely unrecognised by people and as a consequence we remain blind to the syntropic or renewing actions that take place in ourselves, our relationships and the world.

3 — 2 — 1 *Triad of Freedom* (see p. 34). The affirming force is released by the third force. That is why it appears that the affirming force is free. The creative urge is liberated in the world because something new is needed to be born. The transmission of freedom is through the receptive. Freedom cannot be given by an affiming force or transmitted by an affirming force. The affirming force cannot give way. Only the passive can be a medium for freedom.

The child wills to be born and speaks to the wisdom of the mother who draws the father to her. The father is not *caused* to act. He is awakened to his role. No child is forced to enter this life!

3 — 1 — 2 *Triad of Order* (see p. 35). As we have said, the affirmative cannot transmit freedom. But it can and does transmit a pattern. There is an imprinting on the receptive of a pattern which is that of the third force modified and carried by the affirming force.

This is the triad of 'setting up' and shows that in the origins of relationships a pattern (or structure of patterns) is established. *The child is responsible for his own future.*

1 — 3 — 2 *Triad of Interaction* (see p. 36). The affirmative force can have its way with the receptive only through the reconciling. The relation of dominance or authority has to be made bearable and meaningful: this is through the intervention of the third force. In a society it is the middle group that makes it possible for the ruler to exercise his power and the ruled to accept the rule.

In the family, it is the child who renders the domination of the father over the mother a meaningful and workable relationship. *The father tempers his own urges and the mother sacrifices her own inclinations.* In this way, there can be a coherent direction of activity for the family life. Initiative is with the father and leads to change.

2 — 3 — 1 *Triad of Identity* (see p. 37). The receptive impulse has the initiative to do with stability and growth. *The mother wants the family relationship to be more itself.* She develops in the father a constancy and for this, lends him her strength and qualities of persistence and certainty. The transfer of her qualities is done through the child and his power of need.

To summarise, the six forms of the relationship in the family can be named as follows:

FORM	CHARACTER	MANIFEST-ATION	QUALITY
1 - 2 - 3	Expansion	Fatherhood	Transmission
2 - 1 - 3	Concentration	Motherhood	Renewal
3 - 2 - 1	Freedom	Childhood	Awakening
3 - 1 - 2	Order	Pattern	Possibility
1 - 3 - 2	Interaction	Change	Domination
2 - 3 - 1	Identity	Stability	Protection

APPENDIX II

These can be arranged in a convenient diagram

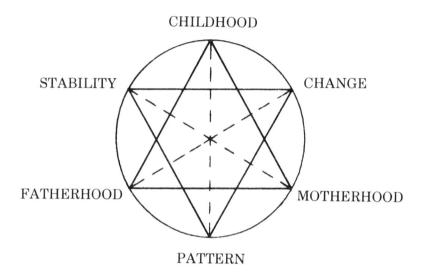

In the complete event of the relationship, all six forms are present and can coalesce into one whole. In practice, some of the forms may be weak or distorted to the point of inversion (negative triads). The condition for coalescence is commitment.

The diagram is, of course, only a convenient device; but it suggests that there is a diverse sphere of activity and function that is represented by the outer circle; a blending of experiences and perceptions that is represented by the six lines intersecting at the center point; and a structure of decision or will that is represented by the star-figure itself.

40-MATCHMAKERS CALLED "ASTROLOGERS"

72- THE FUTURE OF THE RACE - - - -

72- NO CHILD IS FORCED TO ENTER THIS LIFE!

THE CHILD IS RESPONSIBLE FOR HIS OWN FUTURE.

45 FOR THE SENSITIVITY TO RECEIVE - - - GENUINELY NEW - - - - .

GROUP EXPERIENCE

46 HIGER EMOTIONAL CENTER

46 "B". REFERENCE, 48, 48, 53,
   2" (#LWYN)

47 INFORMATION EXPLOSION **AND** NEW FORMS OF PERCEPTIONS

48 DIFFICULT TIMES, FEMALE INTUITION

51 BOZIKS

54 SOUL

55½ EXPLAN. OF WHY I FELT SO TOTALLY BETRAYED BY
   MY HUSBAND

59 IBN IRABI,

57⅝ DOMINATION !

63 PARENTHOOD ! ! !

PIANOJOEHARY = ENERGY OF THE IMAGINATION